MEDICI ART BOOKS

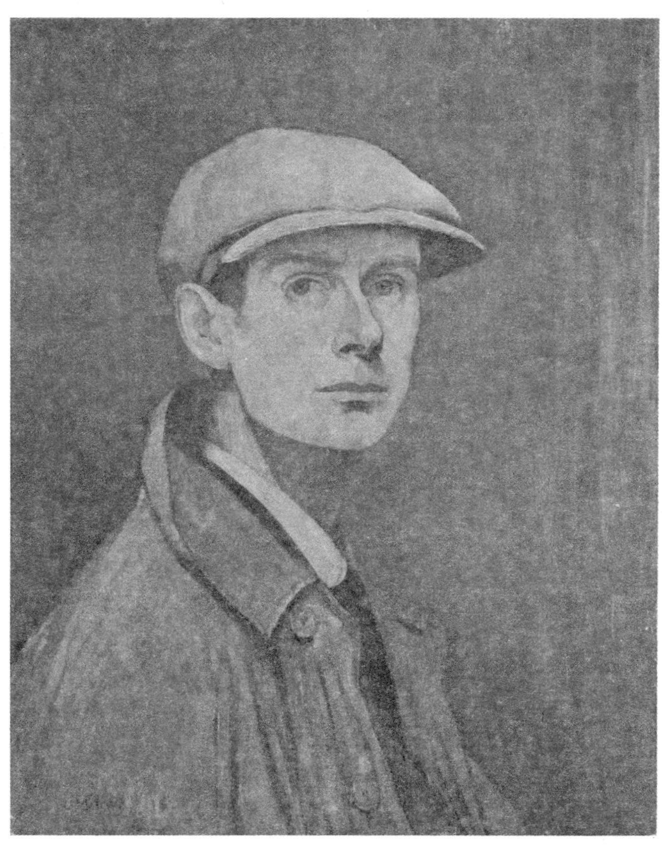

L. S. LOWRY

by David McLean

THE MEDICI SOCIETY LTD
LONDON

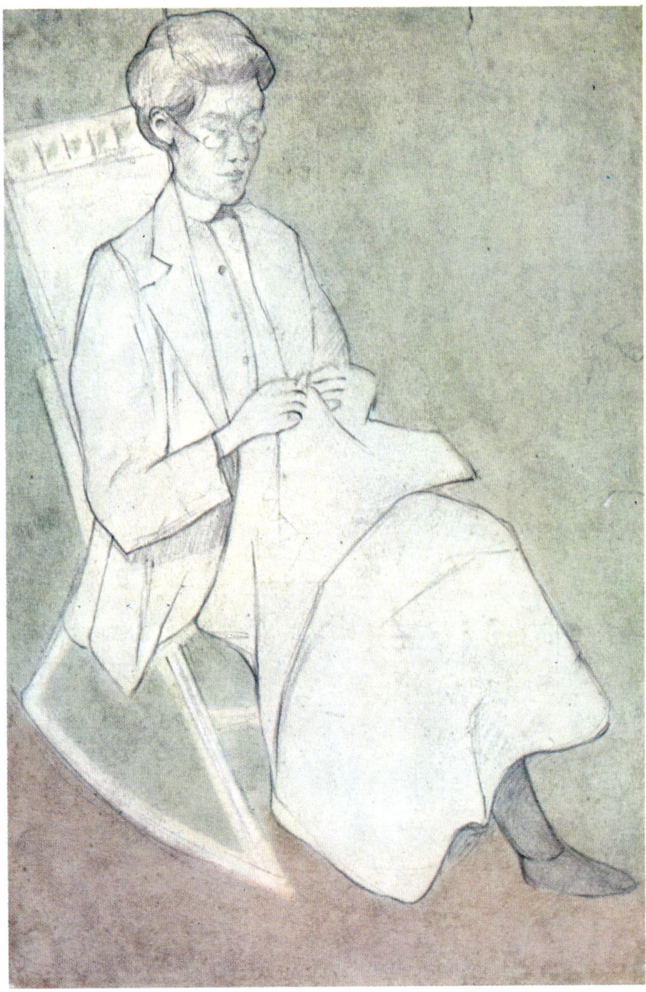

The Artist's Mother, 1906. (Watercolour and pencil.) The Lowry Estate.
Lowry used watercolour only occasionally in his work. He was 18 in 1906 and already a competent artist.

Laurence Stephen Lowry was born in 1887 in Manchester, the only child of Robert Stephen Lowry and Elizabeth Hobson. The family lived in the suburb of Rusholme and when Lowry was 22, they moved to a small house in Station Road, Pendlebury, in the midst of an industrial suburb. His father, an estate agent, was a quiet, easy man, indifferent to his son's wish to become a painter. His mother, on the other hand, encouraged him. She was an accomplished pianist, as well as a collector of china and old clocks. She gave him an appreciation of music which was important to him all his life. Lowry once said of her, 'She did not understand my painting, but she understood me and that was enough. So I stayed on at home, painting'. Neither of his parents made many friends in Pendlebury and Lowry grew up a solitary child.

Pit Tragedy, 1919. Reverend Geoffrey Bennett.

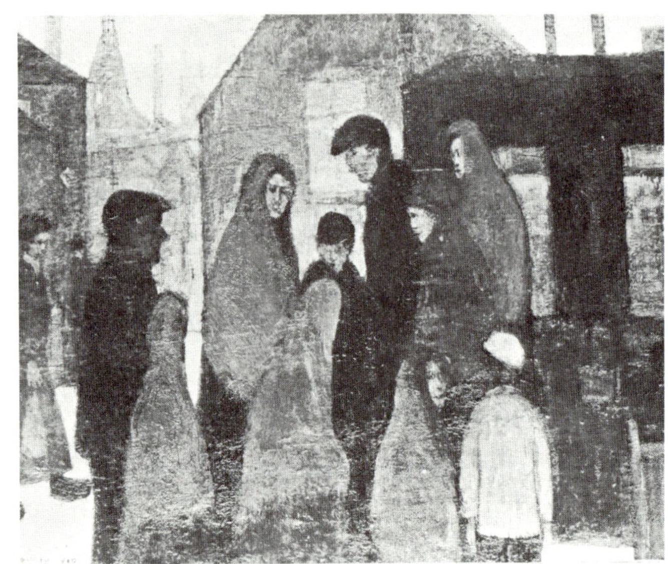

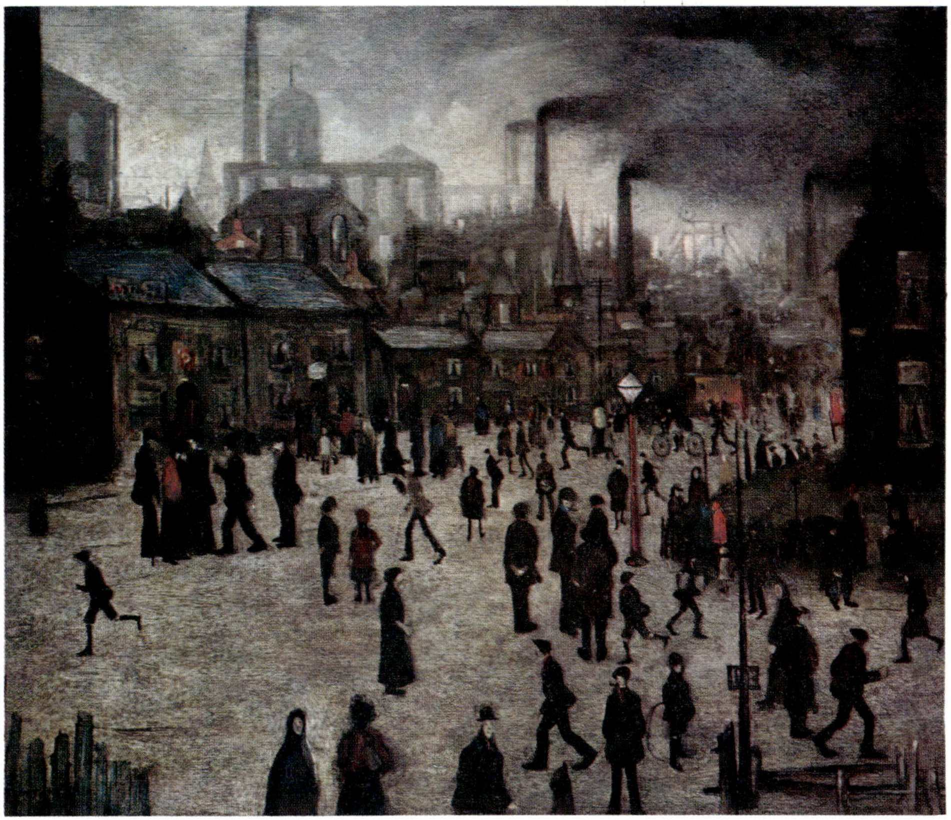

A Manufacturing Town, 1922. Private Collection.
This 'composite' view, showing the choking atmosphere of a manufacturing town between the wars was painted while Lowry's palette was still dark and, in this case, appropriate for the scene. Later his streets became noticeably lighter.

On leaving school at the age of 16 he went to work first for a firm of accountants, then for an insurance agency, and thirdly when he was 22 for the Pall Mall Property Company, Manchester, as a rent collector and clerk at a salary of £2 for a 5½ day week with two weeks' summer holiday. He stayed with this firm for 42 years, becoming the cashier by the time he retired at 65.

Being rather indolent by nature over social life, he occupied his evenings by attending classes in life-drawing and painting at the Municipal College of Art,

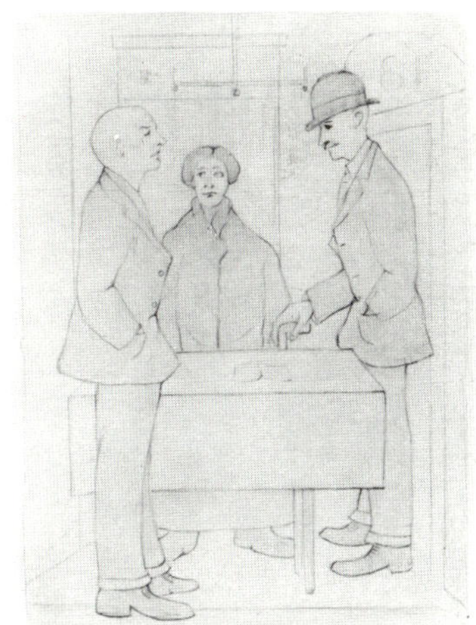

The Rent Collector, 1922. Private Collection.

Manchester, which he continued for 10 years until he was 27. He was influenced by the Impressionist style of his teacher, Adolphe Valette, whose atmospheric pictures of Manchester streets and canals stimulated Lowry's interest in similar scenes for his own work. But in other ways Lowry was a difficult pupil. He failed his exams, took no interest in college life, and was considered an oddity. And yet, of all his contemporaries, he has become the best known artist. One of his few friends at the College of Art was James Fitton, R.A., who made sketching trips with Lowry to Heaton Park and the Oldham Road, and sometimes out to the moors. The lonely moors and isolated farm houses fascinated him; he wanted to remember them, so he drew and painted them.

Between 1915 and 1920, when he was 32, Lowry attended evening classes at the Salford School of Art. He continued to live with his ageing parents in Pendlebury, observing and sketching his favourite streets by day—as he went on his rounds—and painting in his studio by night.

'I'll always be grateful to rent collecting. I've put many of the tenants in my pictures', he once said. He would carry his sketch-book on these rent collecting rounds, and if a street lamp, or railing, or a feature of a house or mill caught his eye, he would pull the sketch-book from the pocket of his old raincoat, lean up against a convenient wall and, adjusting his cap, make a sketch or two. Such sketches were later used in his composite landscapes which he referred to as 'dream-scapes'.

He was drawn to the Oldham Road area between Oldham and Manchester, once known as the most depressing seven miles in Europe on account of the

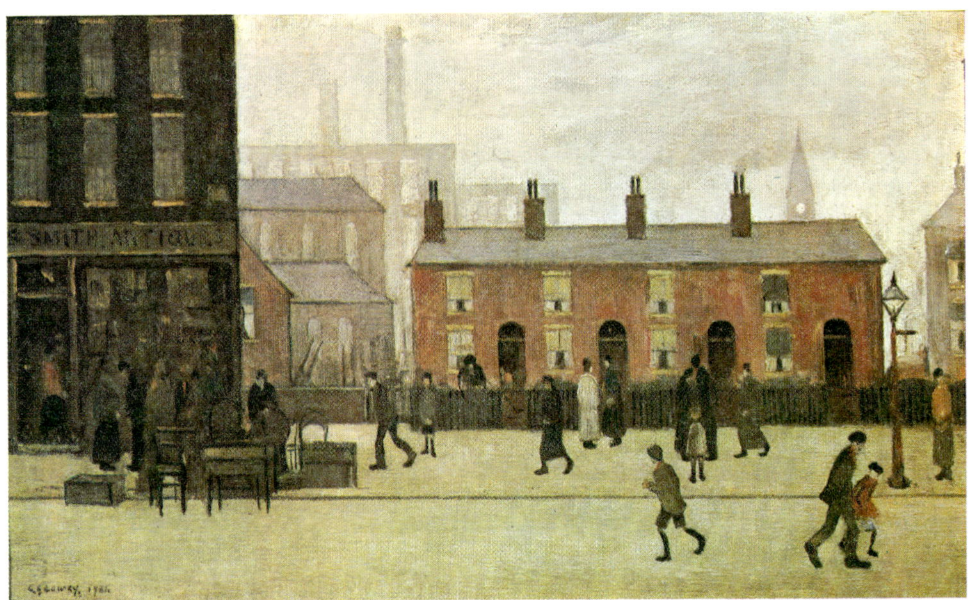

The Broker's Shop, 1931. Private Collection.
Nearly every aspect of a mill worker's life is included in this scene and, during the Great Depression, many jobless workers would have been forced to pawn their only tables and chairs. Lowry shows how many of them lived in small cottages in the very shadows of the towering mills. The conflict between the horizontal and the vertical in art always fascinated him.

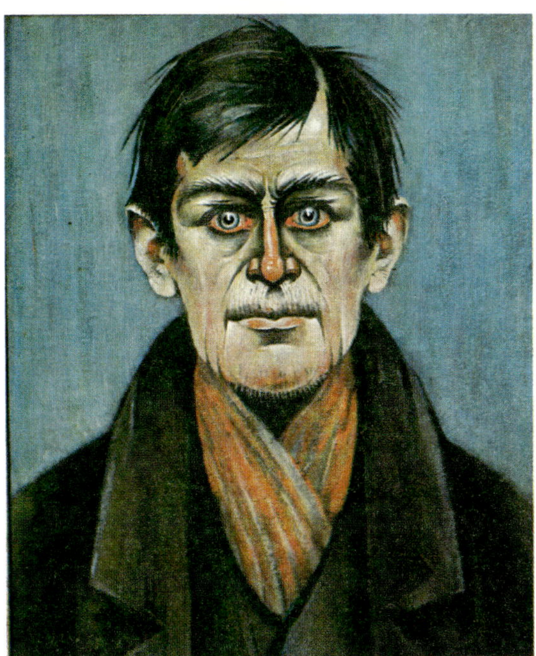

Head of a Man with Red Eyes, 1938. Museum and Art Gallery, Salford.

Lowry, a lonely man especially at this time of his life, was deeply afraid of the approaching death of his invalid mother, for whom he had cared for so long and whose death would leave him with no one. He poured all his emotions into this frightening self-portrait, whose eyes cry out in desolation (see p. 13).

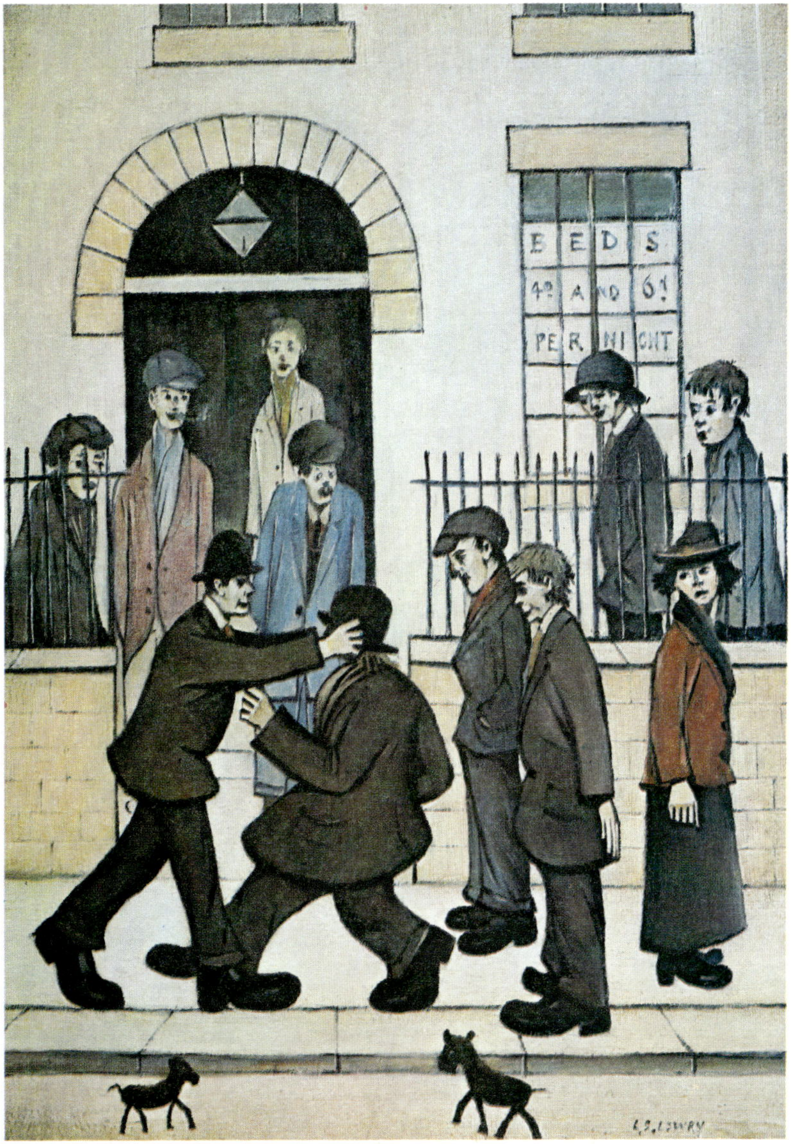

A Fight, 1935. Museum and Art Gallery, Salford.

Lowry would stop and watch any incident such as this fight outside a hostel and would quickly make a sketch. At this time his figures were fuller, and the faces more detailed than in later paintings.

number of mills, chimneys, and workers' cottages. Another favourite place was Huddersfield, to which he sometimes walked across the Pennines, his strong constitution enabling him to cover the 40 miles in two days. Here, and around Pendlebury, Lowry observed the industrial landscape in which he lived and slowly developed a style—a vocabulary of images by which he could describe people and buildings in a way which made them both recognizable for what they were and uniquely his own. By 1920 his style was established.

Lowry wanted to show that in these bleak surroundings there was subject-matter worthy of an artist—and even beauty—an aim which no other painter had made the central theme of his art.

He was struck by the significance of the landscape of these manufacturing towns, the product of the Industrial Revolution and the first of their kind in the world. Here was a whole society of people surrounded by limited horizons—cobbled streets, red-brick houses, little shops, soot-covered churches, chimneys

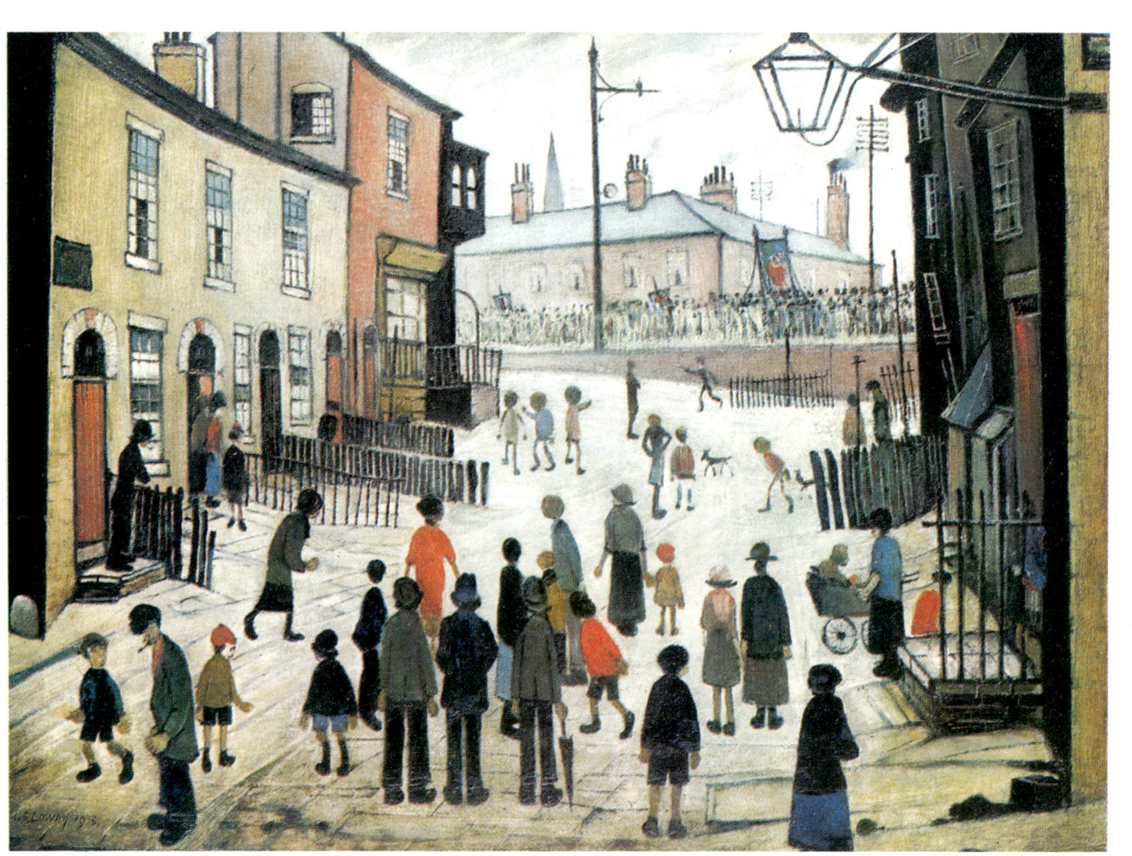

A Procession, 1938. Mrs Vera Kornbluth, New York.
A group of curious onlookers are attracted out of their houses by the noise of drums and voices, and guide one's eye towards a banner-carrying, Whitsun procession which passes by on a raised causeway. Lowry has conveyed movement by making the crowd slightly blurred and its direction by a boy's pointing arm. In the foreground an old man who has seen it all before turns away, distracting the attention of a small boy.

and factories—and driven by the acceptance of their particular destiny of work and play defined by the authority of the cotton mills whose steam-driven machinery set the pace of their lives.

The figures with which Lowry peopled his Northern streets are as instantly recognizable as the film characters of his contemporary, Charlie Chaplin. Some shuffle round in baggy trousers and oversized shoes. Others wave sticks or wear floppy hats. They stoop forward as they walk or stand with legs astride. But whereas Chaplin's figures are gregarious, many of Lowry's are solitary. They go singly and hurry on wrapped in their own thoughts, just like Lowry himself.

Lowry's repetition of his figures is an important characteristic of his work. Positioned with great skill they all play a part in the composition of the whole, often directing the eye to some point of interest. This effect is evident, for instance, in *The Procession* (p. 6) and in *Going to the Match* (p. 13). Lowry gives his figures more significance by leaving space around them and by leaving out shadows, which, he said, would mess up his compositions. So there are no shadows in his work, and no blue sky, even in his beach scenes. All his skies are white, static, without mood. The weather, with its proneness to change, was of no concern to him.

From his earliest years Lowry never seems to have had any intimate relationships and this lack of companionship made him an observer of life rather than a partaker. He painted what he saw around him in terms of his personal vision, unconcerned with what went on inside people's lives or inside the buildings which fill his pictures.

Lowry noticed things that most people prefer to ignore, and was attracted by oddness, deformity and

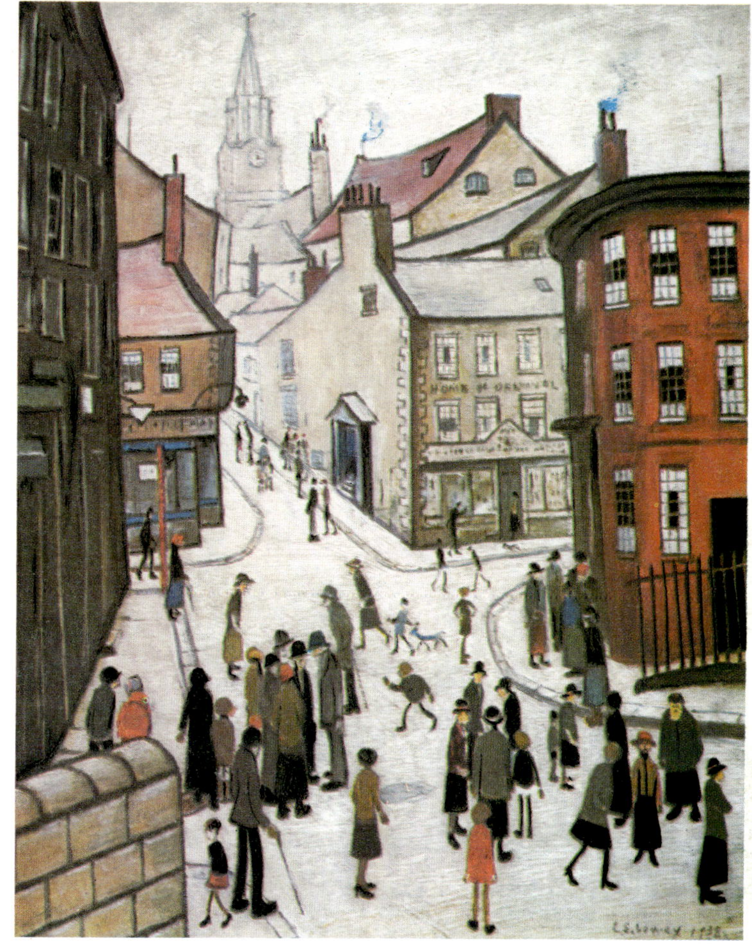

Berwick-upon-Tweed, 1938. This picture was stolen from the Crane Kalman Gallery in 1975.
It depicts a group of people in the neighbourhood in which they played as children and in which they will live all their lives, surrounded by buildings appearing to brood over them through half-seeing windows. The particular place in Berwick-upon-Tweed is West Street, from the bridge end. On the right is the 'Home of Original Berwick Cockles' and, in the distance, the Town Hall Clock Tower.

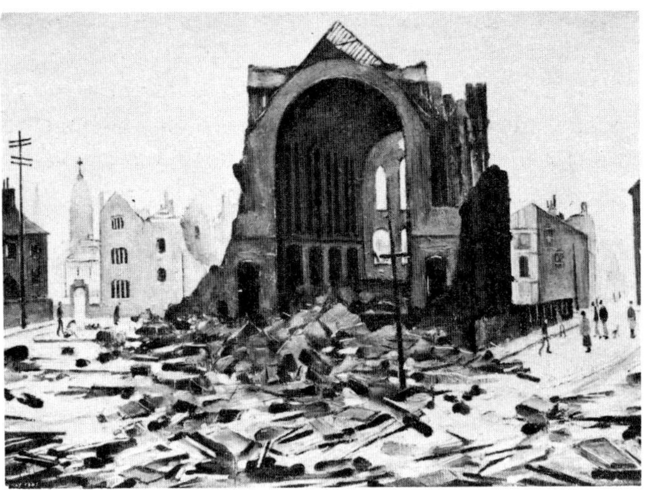

St. Augustine's Church, Manchester, 1945. City Art Gallery, Manchester.
One of several of Lowry's scenes of blitzed Manchester, it provided an expression of his own feelings after the death of his mother in 1939. During the war he was an official War Artist.

events of a grim nature. When he came across fights, accidents or funerals he felt compelled to go and watch. One can learn something about this obsession from the most telling titles he gave to his works: *Pit Tragedy* (p. 2), *An Accident, The Funeral, The Lookers On, Ejecting a Tenant, A Quarrel in a Side Street.*

Lowry's techniques completely suited his chosen subject-matter. Just as he restricted his themes, so he restricted the range of colours he used. Lowry's early industrial scenes were painted in a forbidding grey—grey figures on a grey background of buildings and streets (see *A Manufacturing Town,* p. 3). In 1921 Bernard Taylor, art critic of the *Manchester Guardian* and an early admirer of Lowry's, wrote one of the first and most understanding reviews of his work. In it he criticised his technique and suggested a slight lightening of his 'palette'. So the familiar creamy grey-white backgrounds developed. Lowry became a master of the use of subtle tones of cream and white, giving his work more harmony and simplicity. The process of time was also important. He had a habit of keeping his paintings for years not quite finished, living with and brooding over them and allowing the whites to 'yellow', to darken, and then one day fixing his signature and sending them out into the world. 'So you see', he once said, 'the pictures I've painted today will not be seen at their best until I'm dead, will they?'. Between his blacks and creamy-whites, he employed only vermilion, yellow ochre and prussian blue from which he produced a limited range of soft shades including pinks, rust-reds, cinnamon, ice blue, watery green, and bluish khaki.

If one looks over all the paintings in this book one can begin to appraise Lowry's achievement with this restricted palette, which in itself is enough to establish him as an important modern master. Of course, he did not need a wide range of colours, for the buildings were themselves mostly built of the same few materials: red brick, yellow brick and stone, and Lowry's rendering of their shades is remarkably accurate.

As well as for colour Lowry had a feeling for the paint itself. He applied it with thick brush-strokes and its expressive texture can be appreciated by a close look at an original.

In the 1920s and 30s Lowry was a provincial artist with a job as a rent collector and clerk (see his *Self-Portrait,* p. 1). He was driven to paint by his own inner dedication and as a buttress against loneliness, with no powerful ambition and with little recognition or encouragement from friends, or even his parents. It is related that one spring a girl bought 2 drawings of his for 7s 6d each, and when in the autumn Lowry managed to sell an oil for 3 gns, his father commented, 'If this keeps up, it will be going to the lad's head'. Far from struggling for acceptance, he just carried on from day to day, not worried by the passing of the years.

However, he did exhibit occasionally in Manchester and, surprisingly, at the Salon d'Automne in Paris, where his pictures were accepted on their own merits. He was 40 in 1927 and, although still unknown, was painting many different subjects at this time and used to refer to these years as the happiest of his life. At harmony with himself and with the world he observed, he was painting and drawing in his own special way people and places of leisure; such as games of rounders, public parks, band stands, sailing boats at Lytham and Rhyl— pictures which suggest escape from the grey city centres. But at the same time he constantly returned to the grimmer pictures of black tenement blocks, workers leaving a mill, street quarrels, arrests and accidents. In 1930, he did 12 pencil sketches of the Cotswolds for *A Cotswold Book* (Jonathan Cape, 1931), written by his friend, Harold

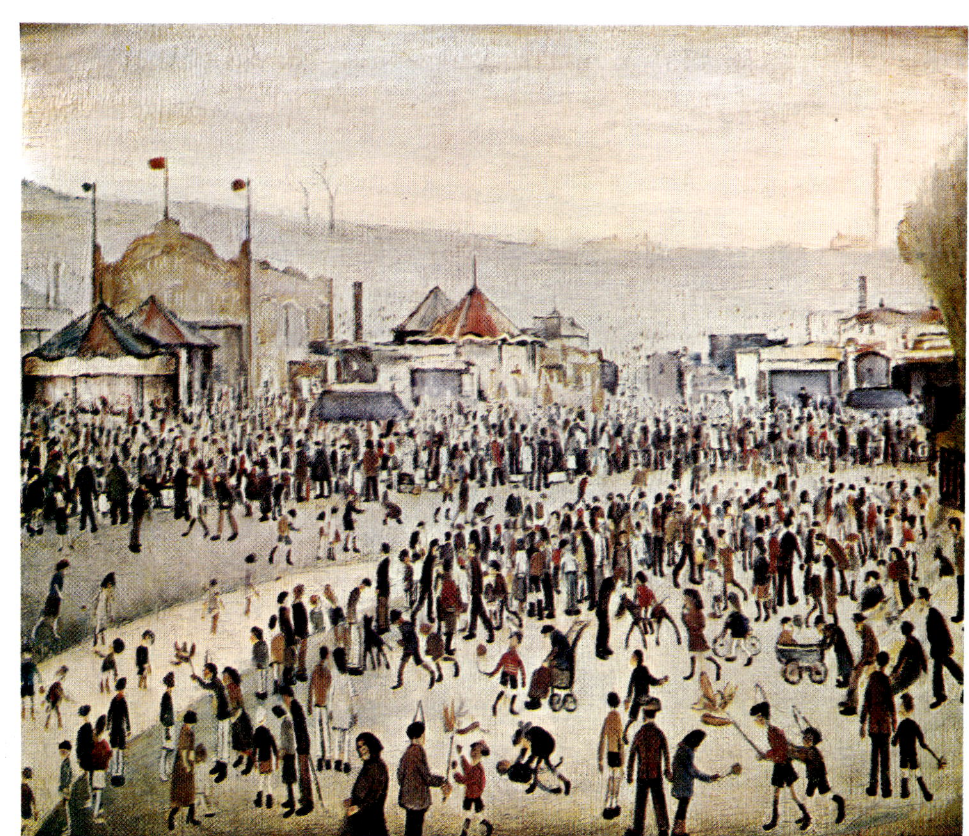

The Fair Ground, 1949. De Vigier Foundation.
Being familiar with the sea, Lowry was conscious of the inevitable ebb and flow of people in big cities, and painted 'tides' of people flowing to and from factories, and at weekends to football matches and fair grounds. In this picture, the fair at Daisy Nook, near Manchester, has become a magnet for Manchester families.

Timperley, choosing some of the more barren and remote parts to which he was instinctively attracted.

In 1932 his father died and he painted a picture of a derelict house surrounded by wasteland—a recurring theme in his work, symbolizing his feeling of loneliness. Indeed, he saw himself as a 'derelict' from a previous age, painting because he had nothing better to do. He often repeated that if he had not been lonely, he would never have seen what he saw. Lowry's buildings seem to echo his mournful detachment, brooding over street scenes with half-seeing windows, almost like abstract faces. Like Blake and Stanley Spencer, he had the strength to brave being neglected and misunderstood by swimming against the prevailing currents. There is no hypocrisy in his work. He painted no false intellectual reflection of himself, but pursued his visions of the industrial scene with tenacity, spending his whole life painting the things that fascinated him the way he wanted, suiting himself rather than any 'accepted' theory.

'They're documents, and I've done them as well as I can,' he said of his paintings, and when someone asked

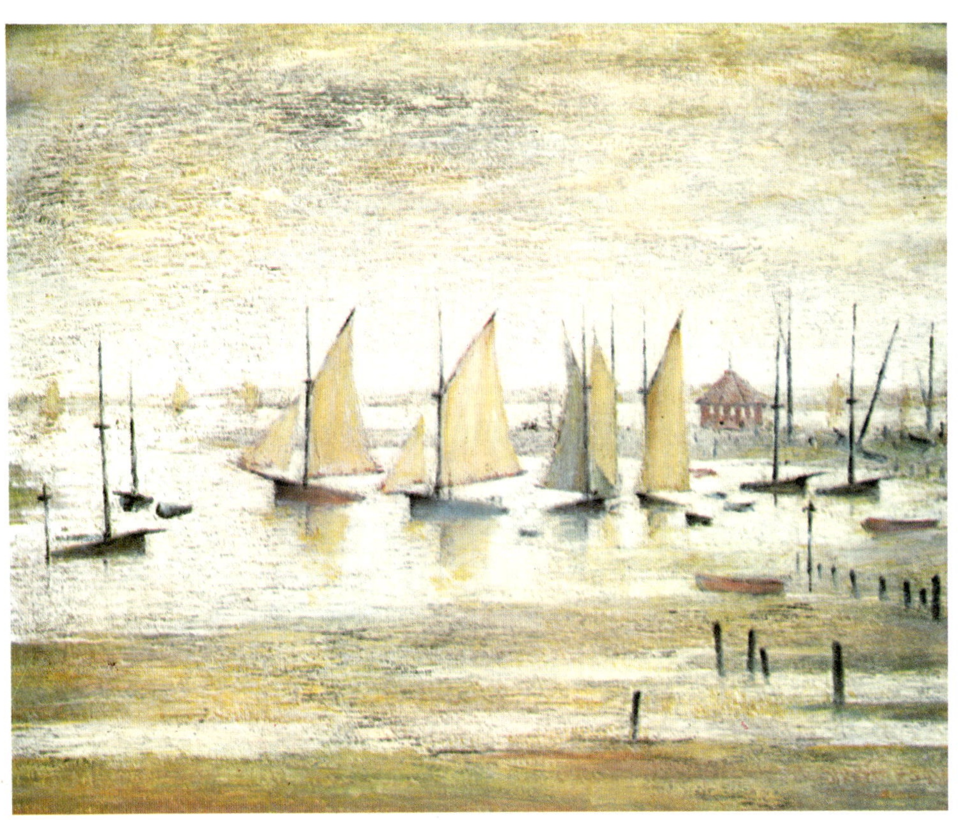

Yachts at Lytham, 1950. Lord Croft.
Lowry's childhood holidays at Lytham and Rhyl gave him a lifelong love of the sea. He painted many scenes at Lytham and here he has found an echo of his mood in these listless yachts which drift on the ebbing tide after the wind has dropped in the late afternoon. Many of the people Lowry put into his industrial scenes would never have seen the sea.

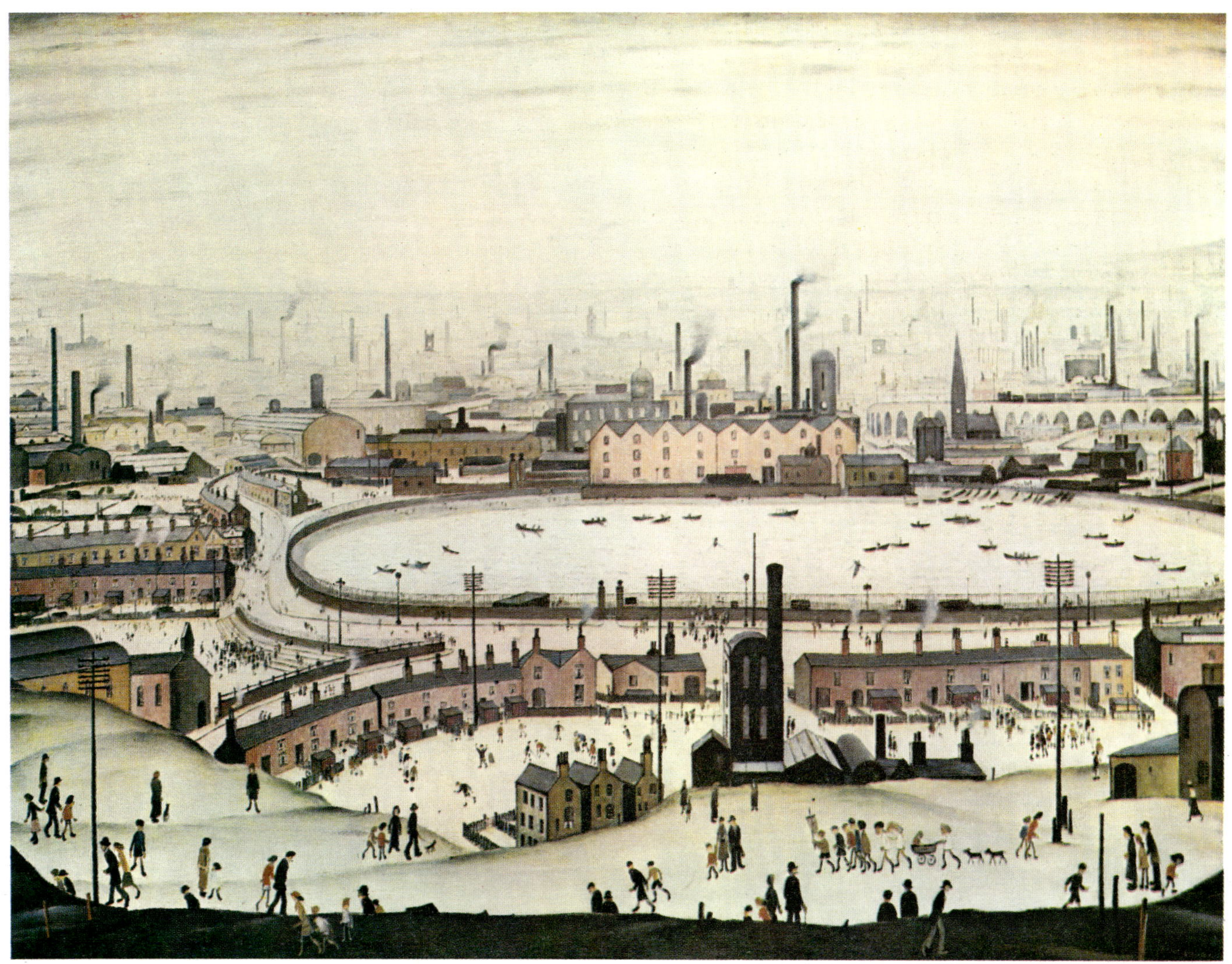

The Pond, 1950. Tate Gallery, London.

This picture contains all the elements of Lowry's visionary language, at its most serene: the raised viewpoint, the barrier across the foreground, the dogs and figures, the incongruous landmarks and pylons, the wilderness of mills, chimneys, spires and rows of cottages, all disposed round an extraordinary oasis—a large oval pond of tiny rowing boats. On the right is the Stockport Viaduct which reappears like a dream in several of his paintings.

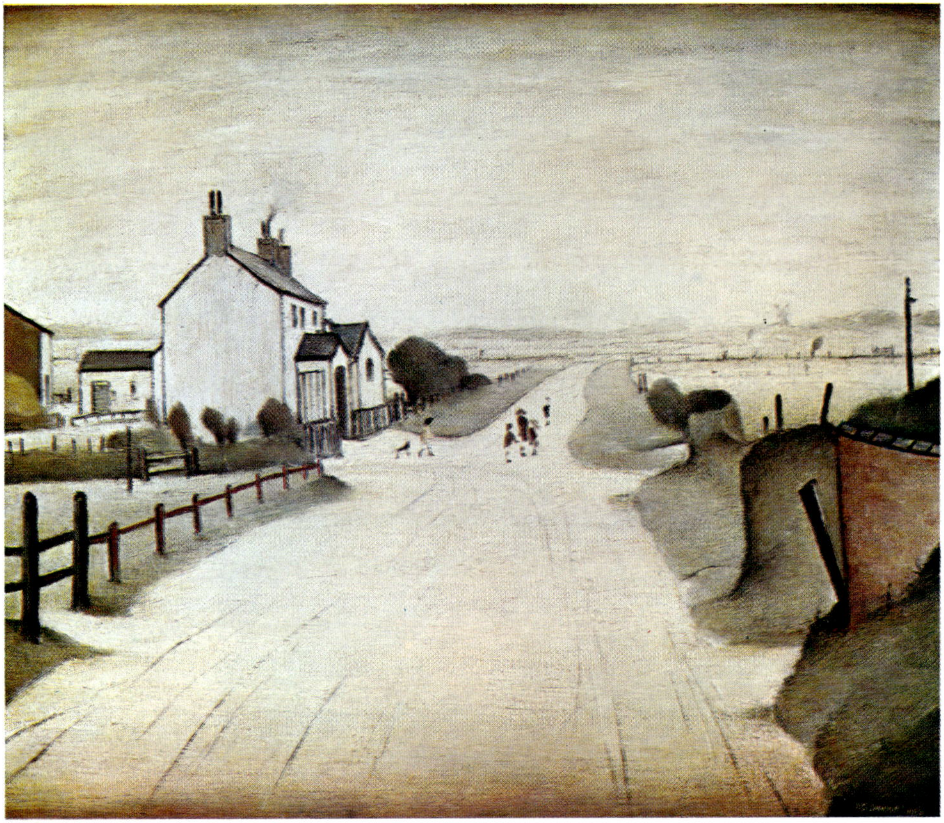

A Country Road, 1952. The Lefevre Gallery, London.
In his country views, Lowry used a characteristic milky green colour and a rounded outline which contrasts with the harder lines of his townscapes. The wide road, the open space and the distant windmill express Lowry's feelings of freedom when he was in the country.

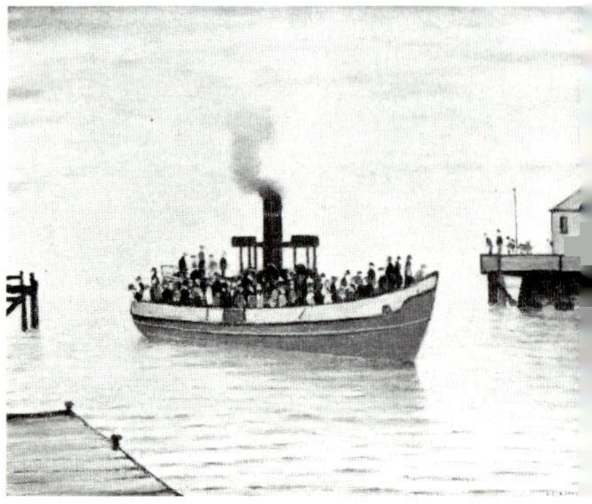

him why his people look like puppets he replied, 'Because that is what we are. We have little control over ourselves'.

Lowry was familiar with literary accounts of industrial life and quoted from Dickens, Mayhew's *London,* and the cynical *Maxims* of Rochefoucauld. However he was not fond of reading and was rarely seen with a book or newspaper. Nor did he participate in current affairs—the rise of the Trades Unions between the wars, the General Strike, the World Slump, the unemployment so acute in his own city. While his friend James Fitton and other local artists were involved in painting banners for the Hunger Marches and designing anti-fascist posters, Lowry was concerned with the more timeless elements of the industrial life of this epoch—people going to the mills or to football matches or just standing about.

Nobody took much interest in his paintings at this time. People thought that for a contemporary artist to be worth attention he had to have taken a current trend a little further; he had to have a following and an influence on art circles and he had to be seen in the galleries. Lowry was not, however, a fashionable artist. His pictures defied easy classification, and as a result people did not take him seriously. Besides, Lowry kept away from the public eye. Ever since his father had died he had been a prey to grief, and, with his mother in poor health at home, was at times close to a nervous breakdown. If he could sell one or two canvases a year that was enough for him and he ignored the few dealers who made approaches.

By 1938 Lowry was 50 and had completed a large number of paintings, some of which were amongst the best he ever did. It was now only a matter of time before a connoisseur with the vision to recognize the art of this unheard-of painter came along. In Pendlebury his mother was in her last illness and Lowry, deeply distressed and with no one to turn to for comfort, poured all his emotional anguish into a haunting portrait, *Head of a Man with Red Eyes* (p. 5).

rry, Knott End, 1953. Private Col-
ction.
lways interested in the sea, Lowry
preciated the beauty of ships, es-
cially the lines of their bows and
erns. By placing the ship of people
ldly in the middle with space
ound it and making it appear
ised between the piers, he gives it
nsiderable impact; and he has cap-
red the air of expectancy that
tends a ship about to make a land-
l.

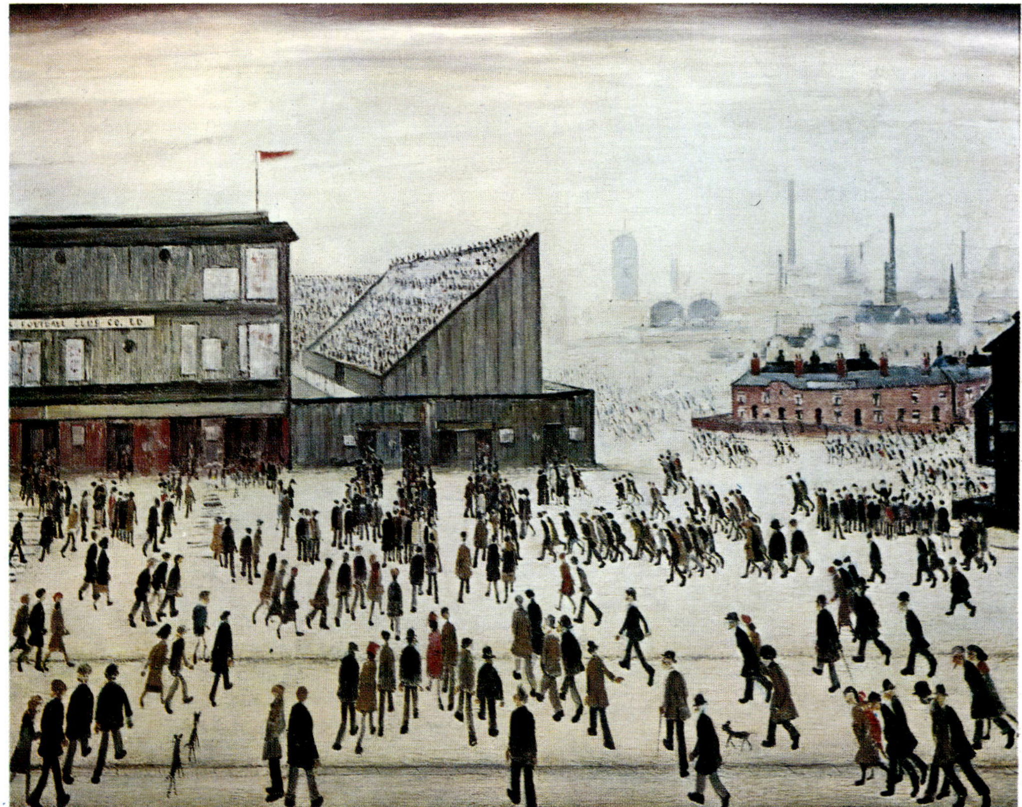

Going to the Match, 1953. Private Collection.
As a young man, Lowry was keenly interested in football and cricket and watched games at Bolton Wanderers' home ground a few miles from Pendlebury. In this composite view, a Saturday game draws the crowds out of the surrounding streets like iron filings excited by a magnet. The entry prices are chalked up by the turnstiles: 3/6, 1/9, 1/9. On the right a man harangues his listeners.

Meanwhile in London a chance discovery led to the end of his obscurity. A. J. McNeil Reid, the London art dealer, spotted some of his paintings at the framers and fine art agents, Bourlet and Sons, followed them up with enthusiasm and in February 1939 gave Lowry his first one-man exhibition in London at Alex. Reid & Lefevre Ltd., who thereafter became his dealers and exhibited his work regularly. This exhibition launched Lowry; his paintings sold, the critics woke up and wrote, the Tate Gallery bought *Dwellings, Ordsall Lane, Salford,* and he began to receive the acclaim he had long deserved.

In October of that year, his mother died. Thus the person to whom Lowry had been so close for 50 years did not live to see his success. She had been an invalid for many years and he had looked after her faithfully. When he was visiting London at the time of his exhibition, he would catch the afternoon train to Manchester in order to cook her supper.

The death of his mother, to whom he owed so much, left him alone and without hope. He insulated himself from the life around him and his mood became increasingly solitary. While enjoying the visits of acquaintances, he kept them in separate 'compartments' and, fearing to be thought dilettante, he disguised from all his full-time job at the Pall Mall Property Company—so successfully that hardly anyone knew about it until after his death.

Understanding Lowry's mood is the key to the interpretation of all his work. He imposed his mood on his paintings thus making them both scenes of contemporary life and psychological statements. But his robust temperament ensured that they were controlled. As a means of expressing his bereavement

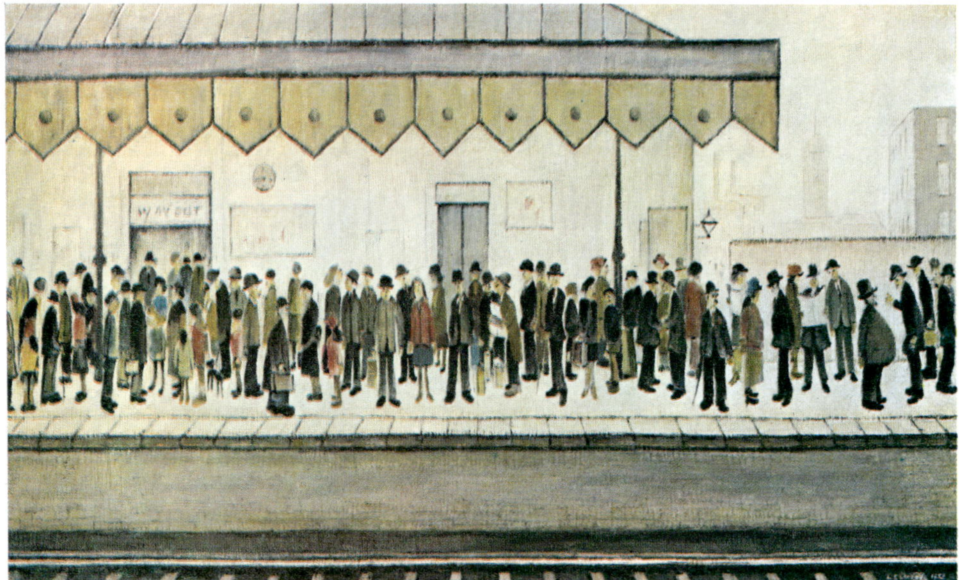

The Railway Platform, 1953. The Lefevre Gallery, London.
Lowry, who never owned a car, often travelled by train. The year after he himself retired, he painted this comment on the inevitable routine of working life. Commuters, each one alone, are hemmed in by the abyss in front of them and the dog teeth above them. Their only way out is on the train, since the door marked 'way out' only leads back into the industrial surroundings from which they have come.

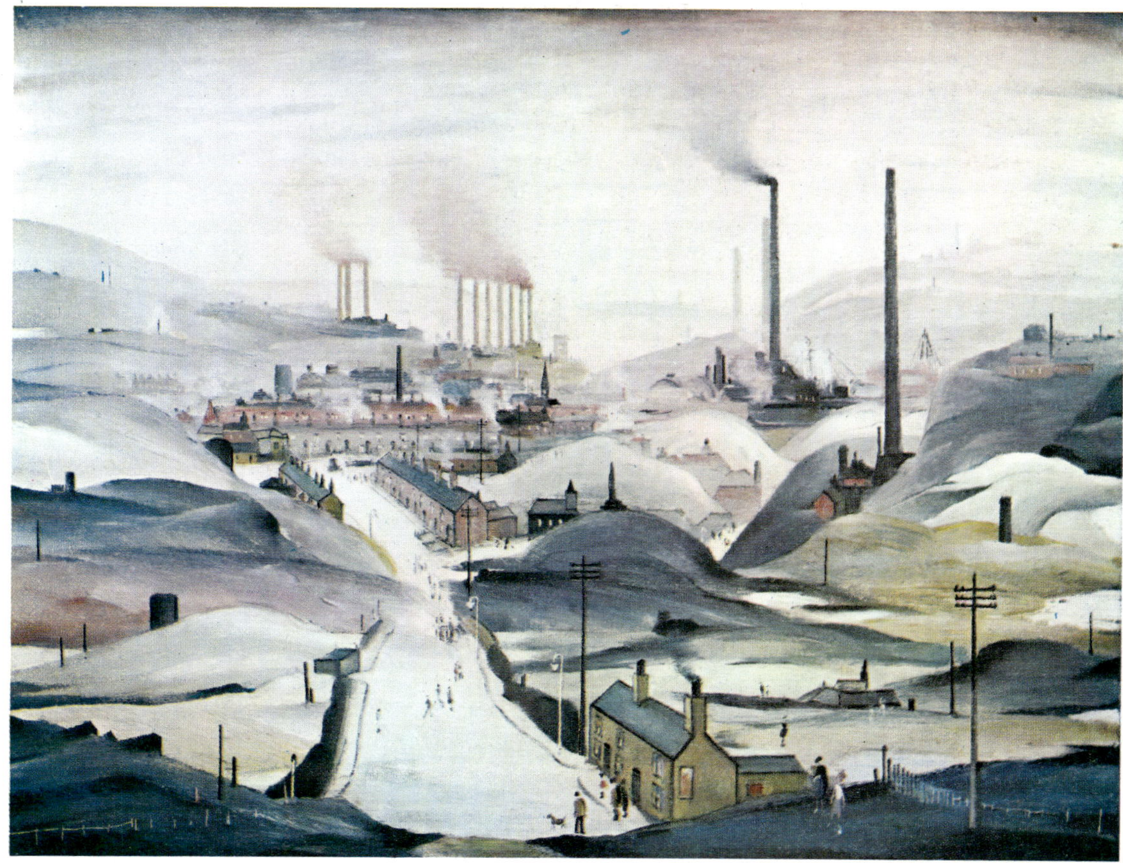

Industrial Panorama, 1953. Nottingham Castle Art Gallery.
Lowry usually began a picture like this by painting a white 'ground' and letting it dry. Then, with only a general idea of the scene, he would start putting in details: a row of cottages here, some tall chimneys there, a mound and a monument over there, building up the picture as he went along and seeing how it turned out. He often put a distinctive barrier across the foreground of his paintings.

in these years he painted several pictures of the blitzed ruins of Manchester—the most poignant being his picture of the dilapidated black shell of a Manchester church, a grim and haunting memorial (p. 8). In about 1945 a different kind of Lowry appeared. Far from the crowded spectacle of factory and mill, Lowry was suddenly on the North-east coast painting, in complete contrast, strange seapieces of nothing except the empty sea and the sky—expressing to all who saw them the empty outlook of his life. A version of the same subject, finished nearly twenty years later, is shown on page 22. Despite this foreboding he had a deep love for the sea and his seascapes account for a high proportion of his work. 'I'm very fond of ships. The sea, too, I love. To watch it is like letting off steam: it's so vast!' Before the war his seapieces were of Lytham, the scene of his first holidays and his earliest sketches at the age of 14. At first the sea was mainly a setting for sailing boats (see p. 10). However, after the war, the sea sometimes became the entire subject-

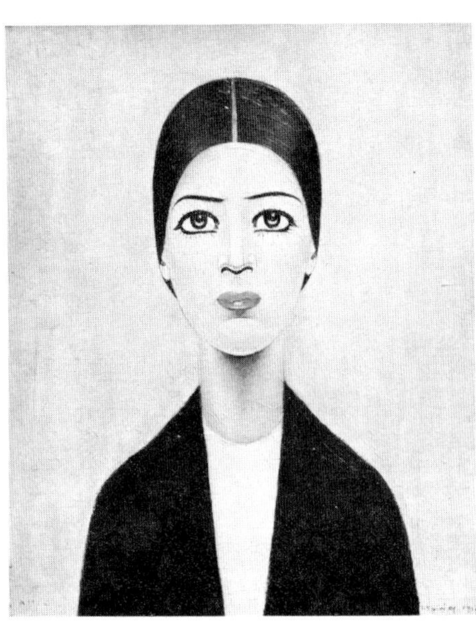

Ann, 1956. The Lowry Estate. Lowry knew several girls called Ann, including his goddaughter, Ann Hilder, an art student, and a childhood friend from near Lytham St. Annes who died young. This expressionless portrait is an unattainable dream-woman reminiscent of the sullen women of Rossetti's that Lowry admired and collected.

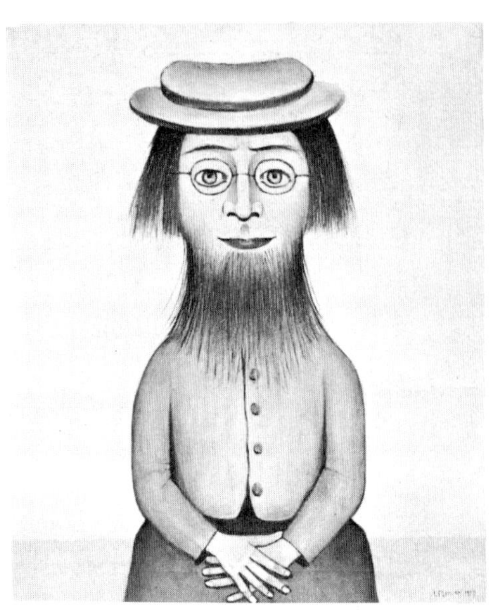

Woman with a Beard, 1957. M. D. H. Bloom, Esq. When a bearded woman got into his railway compartment at Newport, he was delighted. '. . . Well, Sir,' he told a friend, 'I just couldn't let such an opportunity pass so I began almost at once to make a little drawing of her on a piece of paper . . .. At first she was greatly troubled, but we talked, and by the time the train had reached Paddington we were the best of friends. We even shook hands on the platform.'

matter. Harbours fascinated him too, especially the sight of a ship entering—a tiny speck on the horizon growing into a black mammoth as it enters the dock with attendant tugs—and Lowry painted many harbour and canal scenes from this time on.

In 1948 he left his mother's house and moved to Mottram-in-Longdendale on the outer edge of Manchester, near the moors. Despite calling it a 'dreadful place' he stayed there for the rest of his life. He brought with him his mother's collection of antique clocks, which all told different times and kept him company with their random chimings.

Usually wearing a plain suit, an old mac and a trilby hat, he would catch the morning bus into Manchester, spend the day working at his desk or walking around the streets and return home in time for tea in the late afternoon. He would then go into his studio. Surrounded by half-finished paintings on canvas or wood and piles of loose sketches, he would sit at his easel in a paint-spattered suit, his kindly face with its big nose and short white hair turned towards an empty canvas, perhaps listening to the music of Bellini or Donizetti, two of his favourite composers. He would begin with the white ground and no overall plan. Composing from his mind's eye he would slowly build up an imaginary 'vision' of streets, mills and chimneys, often looking through his bundles of sketches for architectural details and shapes. Finally he would add the

Children Playing, 1958. Private Collection.
Lowry liked children and his lanky appearance and mannerisms amused them. He came across these children in a side-street and they happily broke off their street games to pose for him for a moment, while he made a few sketches. The powerful shapes defining the edges of his street scenes are part of his style.

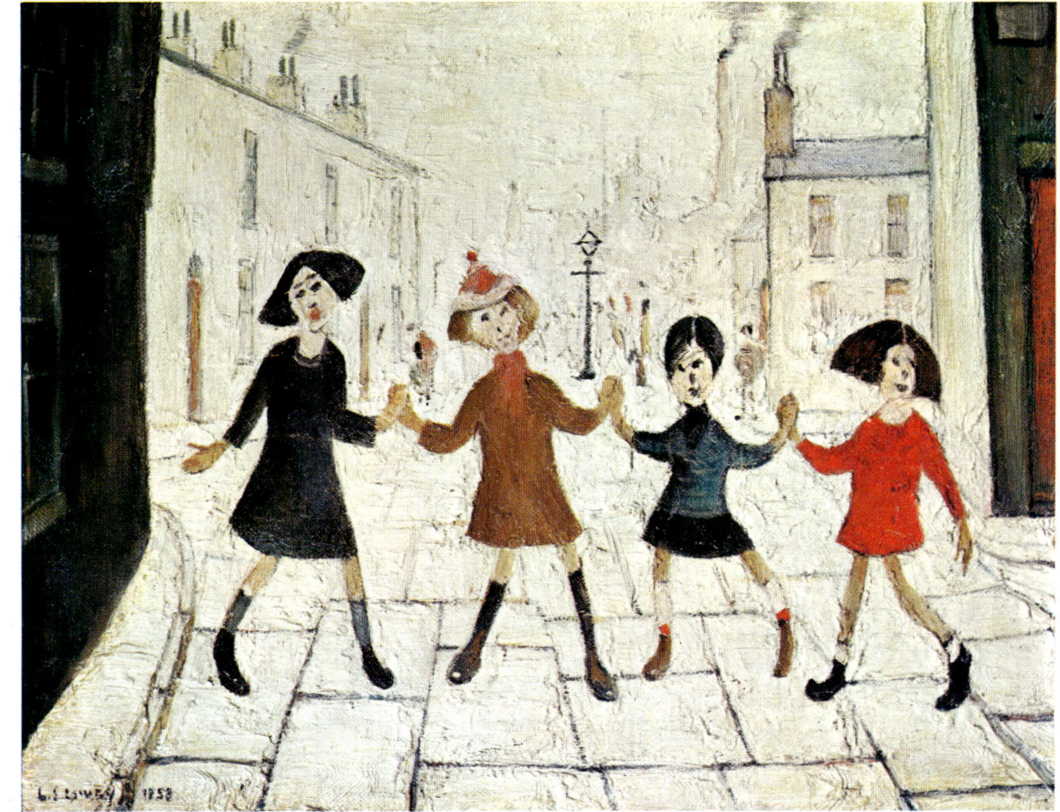

figures until he had completely filled the canvas. Or, if it was not looking right, he would stop and switch to another of the many unfinished canvases in his studio frequently painting late into the night. The less in the mood he was, the better he felt he painted. 'Painting is damned hard work', he said.

The interior of his house was dark and untidy, the furniture old and tattered. His one bookcase and several cupboards were kept locked and the keys conveniently lost. Besides his clocks and china he had a collection of paintings which hung at random on the walls. These included his portraits of his mother and father, and a number of works by Rossetti, whose paintings had fascinated Lowry ever since he had seen them in local galleries when he was an art student. Lowry particularly liked Rossetti's later works, painted after his wife's tragic death and, when he could afford to, bought several of them.

1948 also marked the beginning of public response to his art in his own city. Several years after his reputation was established in London, he was given his first exhibition in Manchester at the Mid-day Studios.

On his 65th birthday in 1952 he retired from his job at the Pall Mall Property Company on a full pension. From now on he was able to travel more widely and from time to time made trips to places like South Wales, the Cotswolds, London, Cumberland and the North-east coast. His growing fame brought him new friends and admirers, with whom he often stayed. As a guest, he was known for his sense of humour, keen observations and fondness for simple food. He loved good stories and had a 'rapport' with children, often delighting them by recalling old hippodrome gags and indulging in mischievous tricks. He also had great shrewdness and awareness of people's ulterior motives.

His travelling in the 1950s and 60s is reflected in a wider range of subjects such as boats (p. 10), beach scenes (*On the Sands, Berwick*, 1959, front cover), farm buildings (p. 12), race meetings, parks (p. 9) and football matches (p. 13). The fields and banks of his rural scenes are a characteristic milky green colour. In London he painted *Piccadilly Circus* (p. 20) and St. Luke's Church, Old Street, after he had been told that it had the ugliest spire in the world.

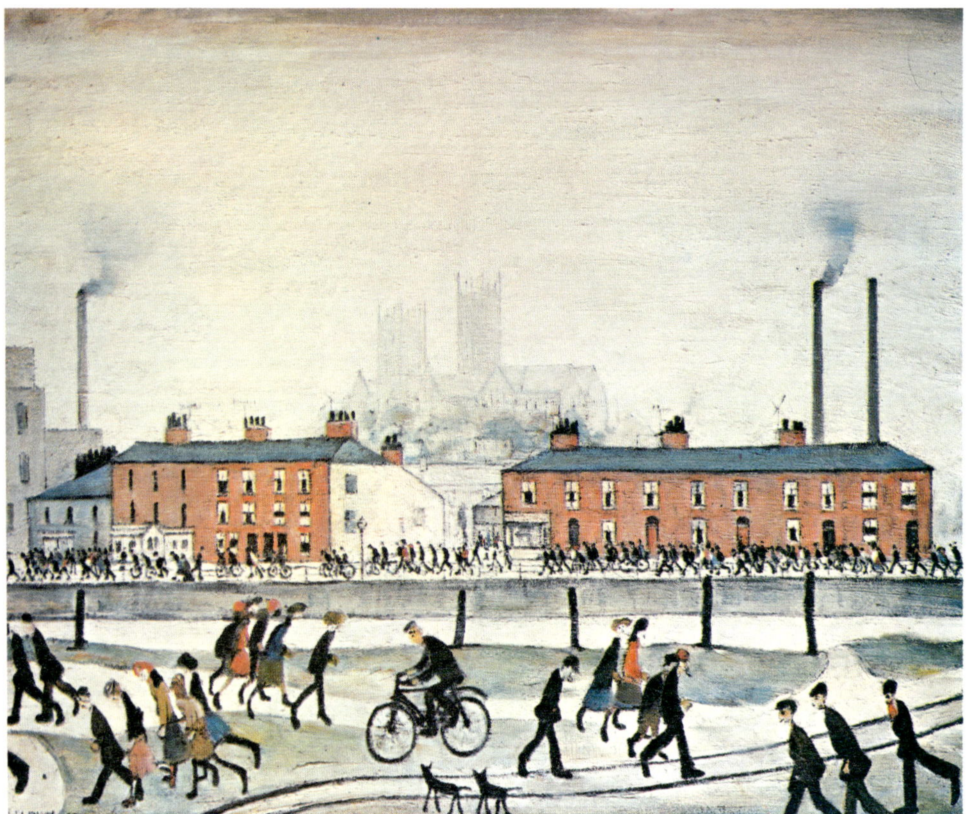

Lincoln, 1950. Private Collection. This painting was commissioned by the owner when he was the Member of Parliament for Lincoln. It seemed likely that the industrial part of the city along the canal, dominated by the cathedral, would appeal to Lowry. When he was satisfied that he was not required to have the cathedral as the focal point of the composition, he agreed to visit Lincoln and found a suitable view by the canal. He made sketches in the twilight when the factory workers were going home. In his first sketch he teasingly omitted the cathedral altogether.

In his old age Lowry came increasingly to identify with cripples, vagrants, and people handicapped in their human relationships. 'They are all people you might see in a park,' he said, compassionately, 'They are real people; sad people; something's gone wrong with their lives.' Starting with *The Cripples* (1949), they became the main subject of many of his paintings and drawings as seen, for instance, in *Man Searching a Dustbin* (1960), *Grotesque Figures* (1970). He was harsh and penetrating in his art and did not suppress the oddness and irregularities he found in the faces of people. This is particularly apparent in his painting, *Woman with a Beard* (p. 16). This interest amounted to an obsession which did not stop at humans; his works abound with odd towers, pillars, landmarks, noticeable for their solitary awkwardness and possibly reflections of himself.

Also characteristic of this 'late phase' (from his late sixties onwards) are a more relaxed style, smaller pictures concentrating on single subjects, and more drawings. He explored problems of communication in such works as *Courting* (1955), *Man Lying on a Wall* (1957), continually searching for ways of expressing the sadness he saw in people's lives. He was fascinated

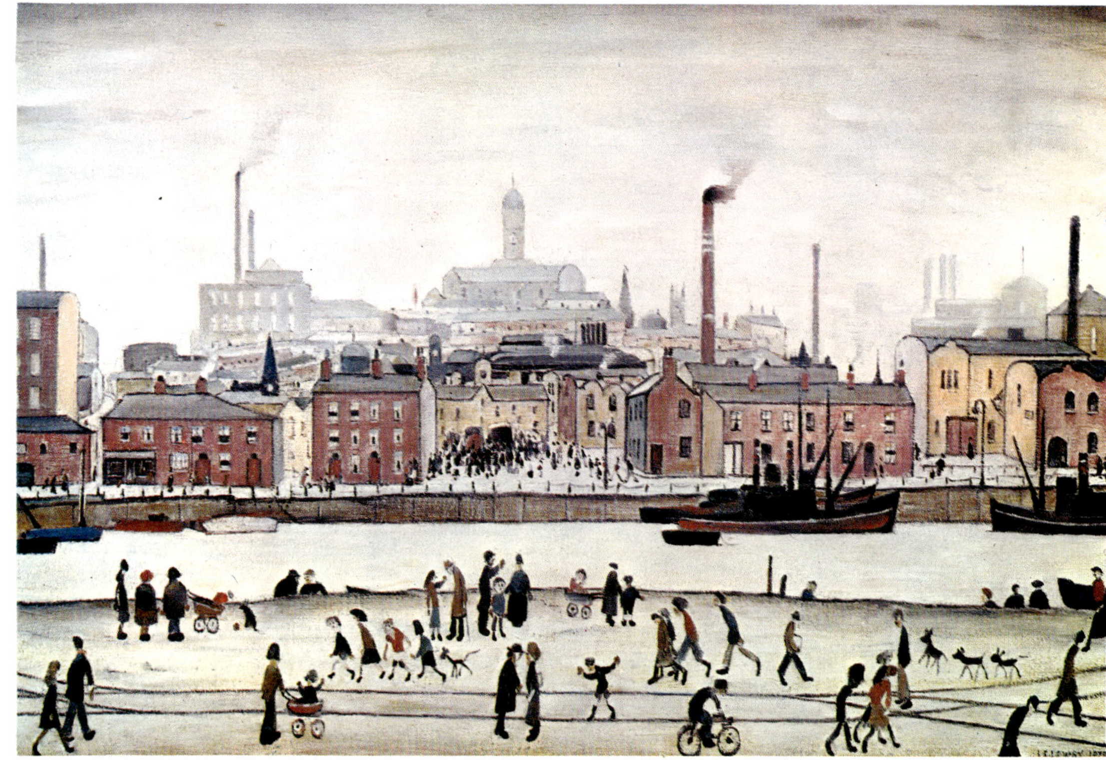

Northern River Scene, 1959. Private Collection.
How Lowry came to create *Northern River Scene* is explained by him in a letter to the publishers dated 11th August 1962: 'A few years ago I was asked to do a picture of *Lincoln* with the Cathedral in it. I chose this part of the River, which is quite industrial, with the Cathedral in the background centre of the picture—later on I thought this setting would make an industrial picture, but instead of the Cathedral, putting in a Factory Building with Tower in place of the Cathedral. I elaborated upon the theme making it more industrial until eventually it came out what you see. But as I say the basis of the picture was the quite industrial nature of the Scene as it actually was.'

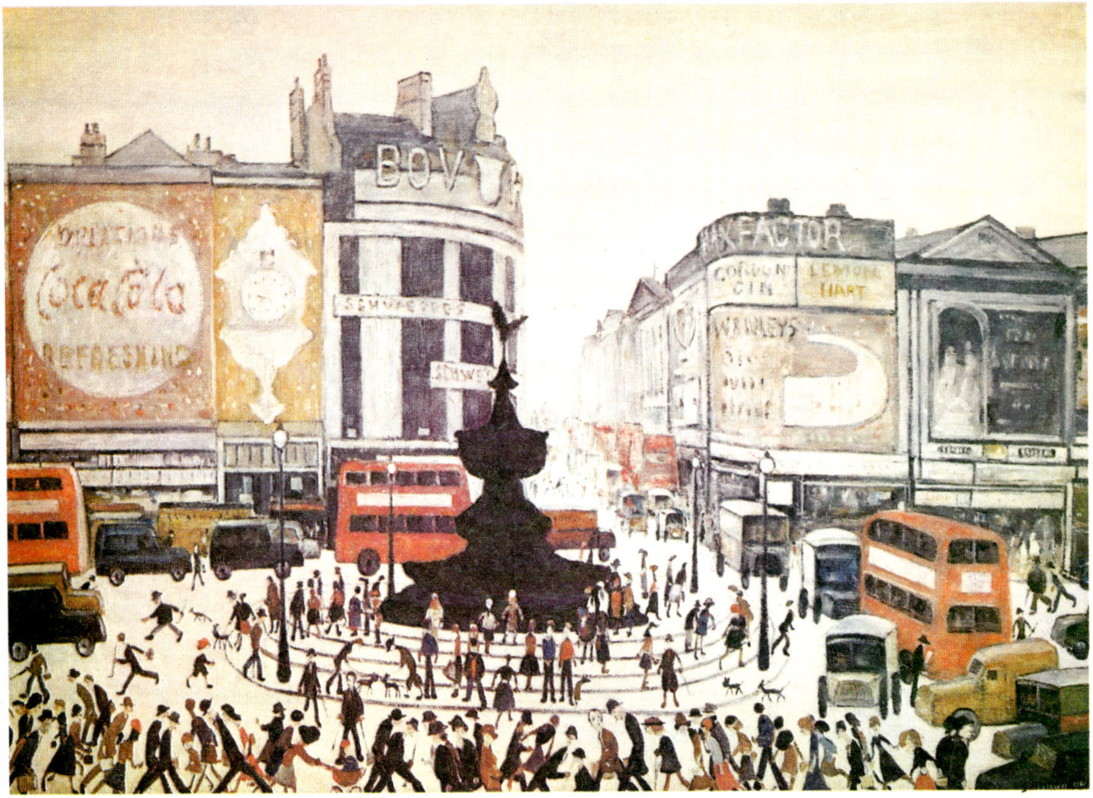

Piccadilly Circus, 1960. Private Collection.
This well-known London view would be painted in a different way by every artist who recorded it as each would in some degree paint himself into the scene. Lowry imposed his own vision onto the scene by painting old fashioned vehicles and the same shuffling figures and dogs as in his Northern scenes. There are no private cars in the scene, or probably in any of his work.

by the idea of people or animals looking at something no one else could see: *Bird Looking at Something* (1964) (p. 24), and his playful imagination is attested by his drawings: *Lady in a Straw Hat without a Dog* (1964) showing a woman shuffling along with her lead disappearing out of the picture, and *Father Going Home* (1962) illustrated on this page.

In the 1960s Lowry made several visits to South Wales with a friend, naturally seeking out the mining villages like *Bargoed* (p. 21). He painted it in a Northern style, but at a distance, as if to show that it was not part of his world.

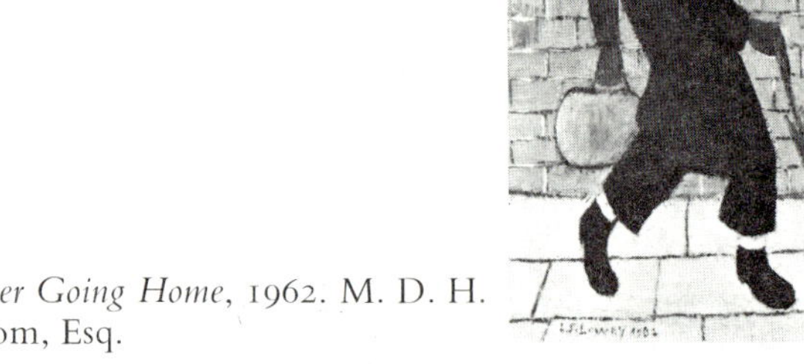

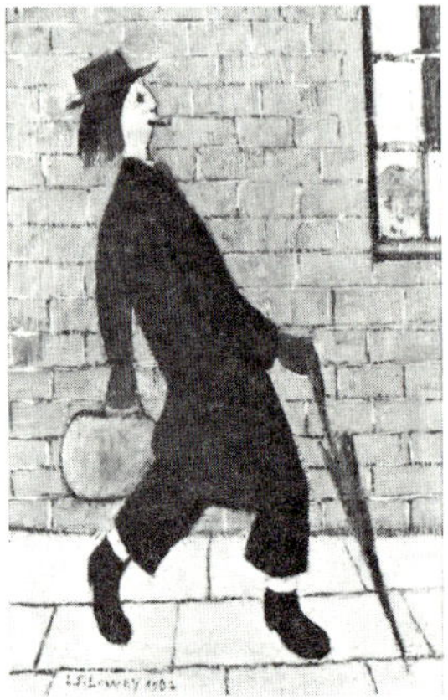

Father Going Home, 1962. M. D. H. Bloom, Esq.

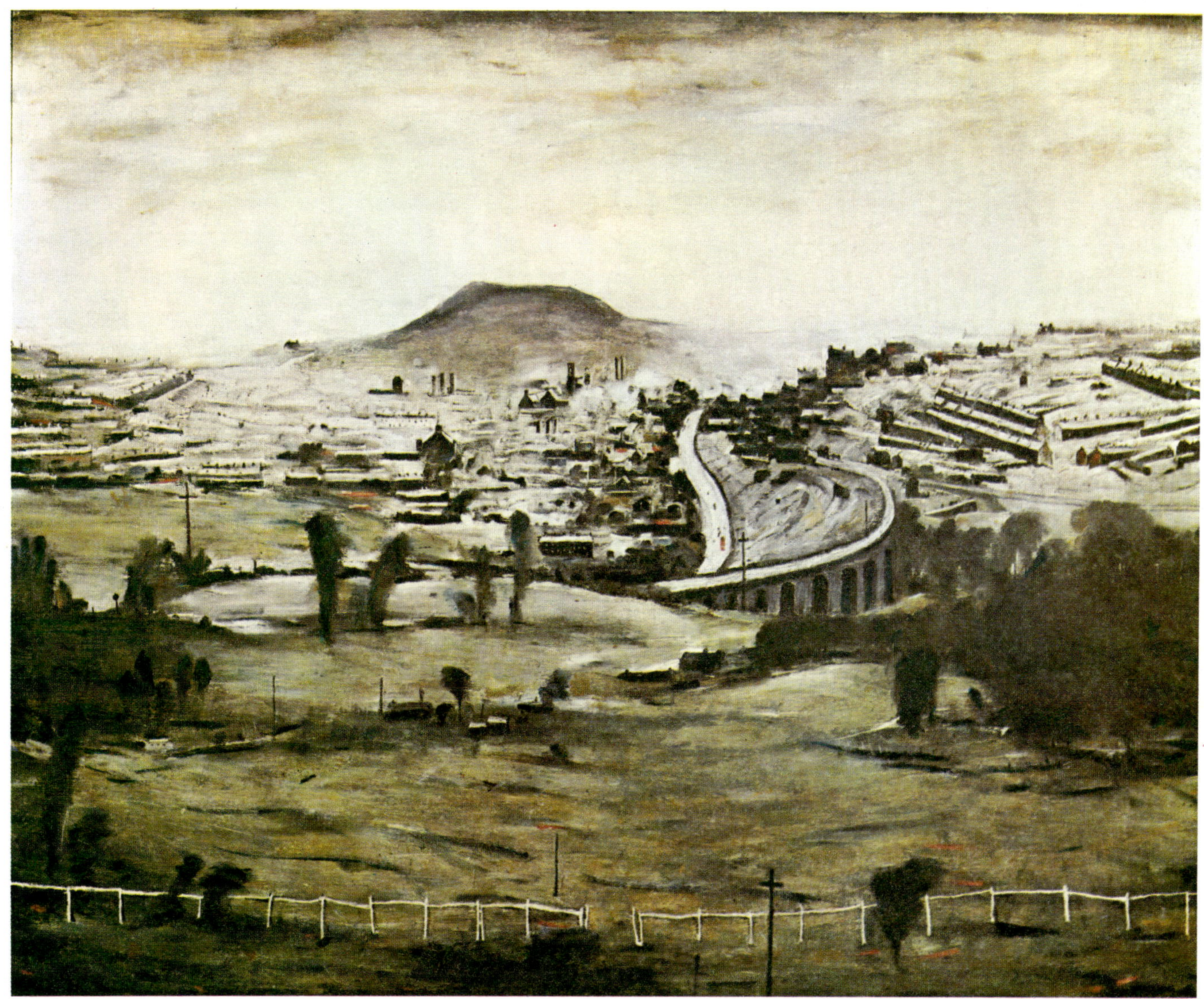

Bargoed, 1965. The Lefevre Gallery, London.
From his vantage point behind a barrier, Lowry painted this Rhondda Valley coalmining town which, sprawling in front of its own slag heap, characterizes the environmental effect of the Industrial Revolution. One of two versions, it measures 5 feet across, and is one of the largest pictures he ever painted. Lowry considered this painting to be an important one and told a collector-friend, 'It is the Chairman of the Board'.

The sea, the longest running theme in Lowry's art, emerges again as the sole subject of some large paintings completed in 1965–6. A gently rippling sea meets a moodless sky at a thin horizon about a third of the way up the canvas. Looking at it, one is disconcerted by the apparent emptiness, and longs for a sign of life. Gone is the sea of beaches and childhood holidays, ahead only an empty horizon.

The psychological statements in his art lend themselves to unending interpretation. As he got older, they became more brazen, and as he well knew what he was doing one can't help feeling that he put them in with inward pleasure. One of his last paintings shows him as a monument. In *Town Centre* (1966) (p. 23), a tall incongruous tower stands amongst a crowd of 'Lowry' folk in the middle of an industrial city and unabashedly in the centre of the picture. No longer a many-windowed onlooking building of the 1930s but a slit-windowed tower in which one luminary clock without hands proclaims that the time is neither wrong nor right, that it has lost its significance. 'Well, Sir,' he admitted to an art critic friend, in relation to

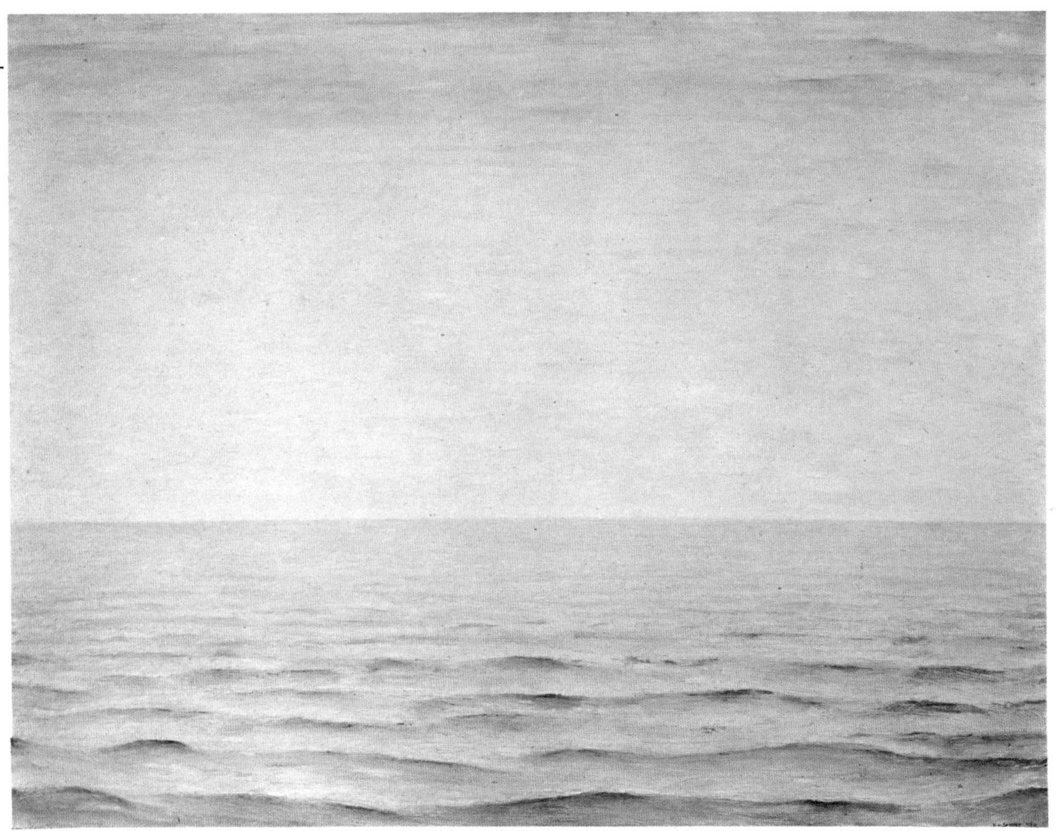

Grey Sea, 1966. Private Collection.
Lowry started painting this theme in the mid 1940s while visiting the North-east coast where he would go to get away from war-time Manchester and the house where his mother had died in 1939. One feels that he was absorbing the solace of the open sea as he painted it.

another painting of 1972, 'I suppose you can say the Monument is me! That's all I am now, you know. A monument to myself! What a way to end up!'

Though he clearly enjoyed the thought, he was belittling his achievement. By now his monument was his work, a total of over 3,000 paintings and drawings, widely sought after and made more widely known through the many reproductions which helped to bring Lowry to a large appreciative public.

This appreciation was stimulated by two important exhibitions in the 1960s staged after he had been elected to the Royal Academy in 1962. A number of leading contemporary artists marked their esteem for him in an exhibition at Monk's Hall Museum, Eccles, Lancashire, in 1964, an honour which touched him deeply, and in 1966 the Arts Council organised a travelling retrospective exhibition which culminated at the Tate Gallery, London. The Post Office issued a Lowry stamp of a painting entitled *Children Coming Out of School* in 1967, and between 1961 and 1975 he received the Freedom of the City of Salford, to whose art gallery he had generously donated so many paintings, and honorary doctorates from the universities of Manchester, Salford and Liverpool.

His own art education having spanned nearly 20 years, Lowry was generous with his advice and help to young art students. From time to time he visited regional art schools, the Royal College of Art, and the Slade, and was fond of repeating that young artists could only paint the places they really knew, where they belonged. To one or two young people he adopted the role of 'uncle', taking a special interest in them and helping them with their careers. All his life he found kindness easier to give than to accept.

During the last ten years of his life, he spent long periods away from his home, sometimes at his

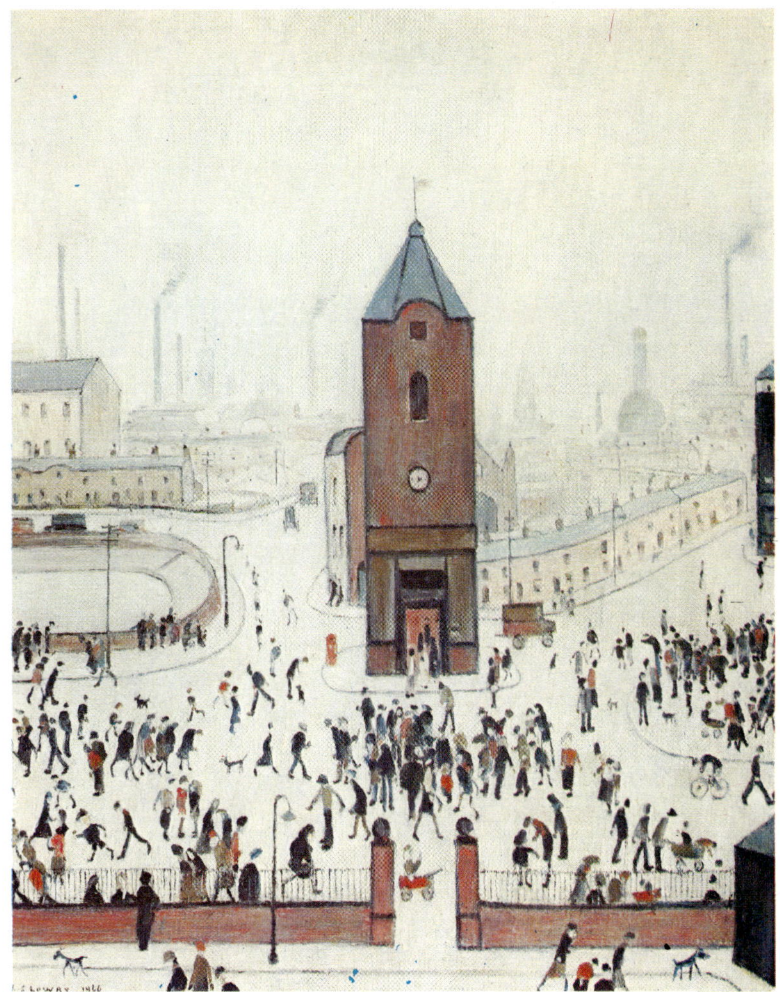

Town Centre, 1966. The Lefevre Gallery, London.
In this, one of his last paintings, Lowry painted himself as a monument. He encouraged artists to be bold in what they wanted to say and not to be afraid of altering perspective or infringing art theory by, for instance, putting the point of interest in the centre of the picture. He called it the 'freedom of the master'.

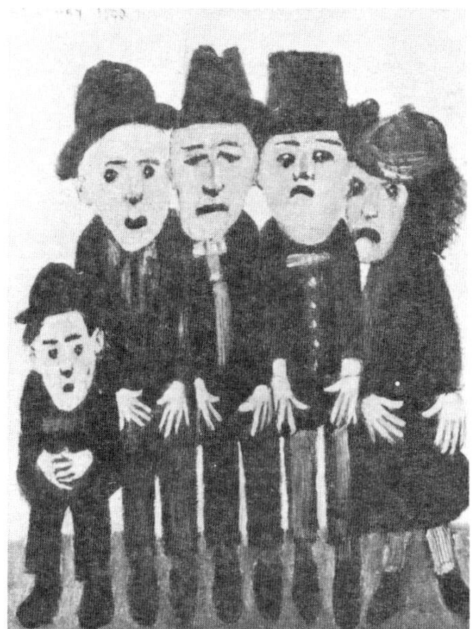

Boy with a Stomach-ache, 1966. Reverend Geoffrey Bennett.

favourite hotel in Sunderland, painting only occasionally. Until he was over 80 he never lost his vigour or his artist's eye and, despite saying he was giving up, continued to draw until a few months before his death. Lowry's way of life was hardly touched by his belated fame and fortune. His house remained untidy and his suits shabby to the end. He only had a telephone at the end of his life; he never went abroad, or owned a motor car, and his only known indulgence was the occasional ride across England in a Manchester taxi, on one occasion turning up at a distant friend's house wearing his carpet slippers. In February 1976 at the age of 88, he died after a short illness, seven months before a major retrospective exhibition of over 300 works was put on at the Royal Academy in London.

So the Pendlebury artist, at first so lonely and who remained overlooked and unpraised for so long and even when fame arrived continually asked, 'Was it worth it?, Will I last?' died knowing that he was being given an honour accorded only to England's most acclaimed artists.

It has been said that Lowry, stimulated by an affection for the place and its people, transformed the ugliness of the Northern streets into a fairyland without telling lies about it, but Lowry himself firmly believed that the quality of beauty was there and that nobody would have seen it unless he had painted it.

Bird Looking at Something, 1964. M. D. H. Bloom, Esq.

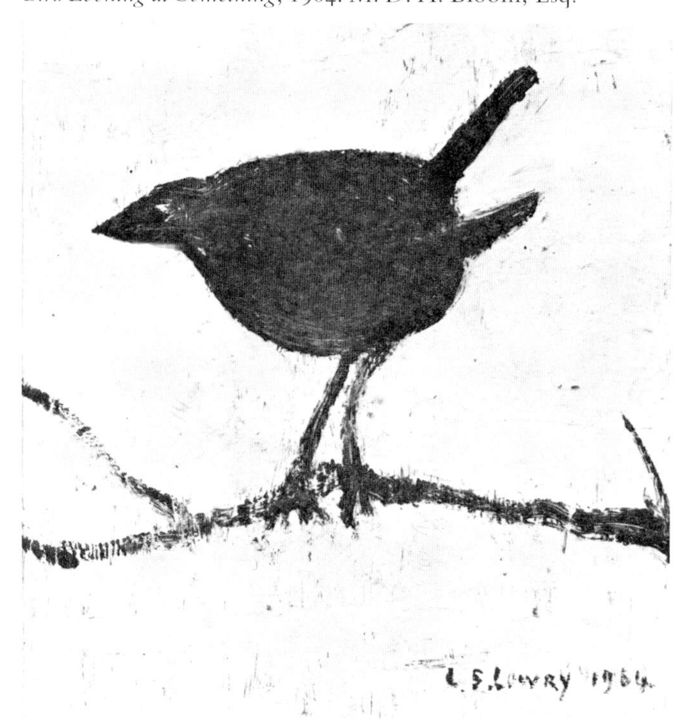